Thread and Nectar

poems by

Mobi Warren

Finishing Line Press
Georgetown, Kentucky

Thread and Nectar

Copyright © 2020 by Mobi Warren
ISBN 978-1-64662-283-2 First Edition
All rights reserved under International and Pan-American Copyright Conventions. No part of this book may be reproduced in any manner whatsoever without written permission from the publisher, except in the case of brief quotations embodied in critical articles and reviews.

ACKNOWLEDGMENTS

Blue Lyra Review: Sesame Seeds Pray (short poem winner)
Broken Circle (anthology), Cave Moon Press: Ingredients
Is This Forever, or What? (anthology), Greenwillow Books: Squirrel's Hands
Love Poems to San Antonio (anthology), San Antonio Department for Culture and Creative Development: San Anto Persimmons
Poets Against the War website: One Hundred Thousand, 2003
San Antonio Express-News: Rosary, Summer Tomatoes
Texas Poetry Calendar: Sandhill Cranes at Salado Creek
The Enigmatist: Atmosphere (in a previous version titled Once)
Thirty Days (anthology), Tupelo Press: Early Morning Runs that Became Rescues
Voices de la Luna: Ceremony for the Cynipid Wasp; Fracking the Eagle Ford; Mole Negro de Oaxaca; Phantom; Spira Mirabilis

Publisher: Leah Maines
Editor: Christen Kincaid
Cover Art: Norma Jean Moore, www.normajeanmoore.com
Author Photo: Emily Han
Cover Design: Elizabeth Maines McCleavy

Order online: www.finishinglinepress.com
also available on amazon.com

Author inquiries and mail orders:
Finishing Line Press
P. O. Box 1626
Georgetown, Kentucky 40324
U. S. A.

Table of Contents

Squirrel's Hands 1

Rosary 2

Atmosphere 3

Fracking the Eagle Ford 4

Jizo's Heart 6

Cypress at the Blue Hole 8

Papel Picado 10

Epiphany 12

Ceremony for the Cynipid Wasp 13

Flight Surgeon 14

Cranes at Aransas Pass: Quilt Square for 350.org 15

Early Morning Runs that Became Rescues 16

One Hundred Thousand, 2003 17

Sesame Seeds Pray 18

Empathy for the Diamond Ant 19

Phantom 20

Ingredients 21

Arrival 22

Sandhill Cranes at Salado Creek 23

San Anto Persimmons 24

During the City Nature Challenge 25

Summer Tomatoes 28

Mole Negro de Oaxaca 29

Spira Mirabilis 30

Black Rose 31

Squirrel's Hands

My aunt used to say she wanted to come back
a tiger in her next life.
My father said he would return an eagle.
My mother preferred something small and simple,
a sparrow.

Grandmother crossed over without ever saying,
but recently I have spotted her.
She is a squirrel living close by.
She measures acorns that resemble thimbles
and raises mast to scissor teeth.

Already she senses
        the heartbeats
                of life continuing
                        beyond her

When she sewed, the exact gestures of my grandmother's hands
were like a squirrel's examining hickories and walnuts.
She did not cut thread so long it tangled
for she knew its umbilical weight.

The cloth in her hands acquired vibrato;
each stitch pulsed with apt and supple care.
She did not have to say
I will return a squirrel.
She knew I would recognize her hands.

Rosary

Repeating holy words
to the count of beads,
we clean our hearts.

My eyes rest
on the bead-like body
of a hummingbird,
color of dust
in dappled shade.
Perched on a twig,
direct line of sight
to the sugar feeder,
thin beak preens
in blurs,
wings vibrate clean.

In our own way,
we shuffle strings of olive pit,
filbert, even bits of polished bone
between thumb and finger
to enter
        stillness,
another sip of nectar.

Atmosphere

       i

Down one aisle,
an expiration date
is printed on the label
of the *All-Natural Dog Treat,
Sterilized Beef Bones:
Product of Brazil.*

Cattle who stood
on these scrubbed shin bones
grazed on the stubble
of rainforests.

You've seen their docile faces.
And the grateful dog
does not know she holds
the earth's lungs
in her fangs.

      ii

Once
under another Big Box
in the marrow of limestone caves,
silent albinos—rare blind beetles,
eyeless spiders, lived.

Before the ground above them sealed,
raindrops wiggled through rock,
fell into secret pools with the plink
of xylophone or harp.

Jointed bodies of spun glass
hinted light, defined thin lines
of existence suited to this
one place, once.

Fracking the Eagle Ford

In a dream I held four
pebbles in my mouth
to slake thirst during a hundred-year drought.
Four words,
syllables of the sacred.
I awoke singing
Hymen
Hymenoptera
Foramen
Foraminifera
and wanted to dance a Circle
over the Eagle Ford Shale
to cleanse what we have done.

Children born in a time of shattered rock
and the reckless burn of carbon,
forgive us.

Hymen
We force Water, Giver of Life, into a weapon
to sunder the Mother's hidden membranes.
We plunder glittering fossil beds,
foraminifera,
the ancient reefs beneath our feet.
We are grave robbers
who burn cradles.

We forsake the wild bees,
hymenoptera, community-minded insects,
whose dance of take is also a dance of give back.
We erase their courtship
of horsemint and paintbrush,
star-faced phlox—
flowers powered by the sun
whose spidery roots find paths
through rock
by becoming one with it.

Foramen
For the Children *Amen*
Hold a newborn in your arms.
Place a light hand over the pulse
at the crest of her skull, the soft spot
where hint of sea still murmurs,
child swathed in wonder.

She cries for clear water,
unmolested land, untainted air.

Jizo's Heart

Jizo's heart is a bag of stones.
Drawstrings pulled tight
leave a small mouth.
Press a finger lightly there
and the bag opens
like an infant's mouth
to a mother's breast.

Jizo swallows stones
as a snake does eggs,
the origin
of stacking stones
on children's graves.

Rabbis know this custom.
Pebbles pile
like children's shoes
at Auschwitz,
shoes of cracked leather
and tongues of dust,
once brown as chestnuts,
polished as apples.
Notches on the laces,
an alphabet of loops,
a child's first cursive
folded over the foot.

In Hiroshima,
smooth stones mime
Sadako's hands
cutting squares of paper
and folding cranes;
A thousand could
remove the bomb's
fire from her bones.

Friends saved papers
that wrapped eggplant
or bamboo. Her father,
papers from his barbershop,
until her thin hands followed
the cranes' flight home.

Measured in shoes
and origami birds,
a child's despair
is inseparable from hope.
Like the children's game
of dropping small stones
into cups on a playing board,
the patter of grey granite
echoes in the nest
of Jizo's heart.

* In Japanese Buddhism, the bodhisattva Jizo is the Guardian of Deceased Children

Cypress at the Blue Hole
for Dora

Winter

All winter I watched
the plain grace of your hands
as you knit a shawl,
cochineal-dyed wool
spun in Mexico.
I held it to my face,
inhaled the earthy tang,
all the tiny beetles
swathed in white,
scraped from cacti,
crushed for red.

We sat at my table
over bowls of soup,
squash and roasted pear,
toasted bread.
Your hands drew paths
as you spoke
as if to trace moths
drawn to moon.

You were tired,
you had danced all day,
given ceremony on the riverbank
by the stubbled knees
of silver cypress.

When I hugged you at the door
there was something else,
a sudden dropping away
within you, an absence
before it is named.
I felt it in my arms
and wanted to hold you longer.

No one could have guessed
      not even you
who lived in the wisdom
of your body.

Summer

Your daughters place
origami peace cranes
on the branches
of a cypress sapling,
planted here to root you
by the clear blue spring
where the river emerges,
pecans and prickly pears
to nourish you,
drum and bone whistle,
scent of burning copal.

Fireflies weave
between the grasses,
your daughters move like you.
Here you are, dancing.
Bone and ash
ride the river to the sea.

Papel Picado

Late afternoon
        on the Day of the Dead
the cedar elm
        rises by the porch
wielding chisels
        of fine-toothed leaves,
brittle and gold
        as burnt sugar.
They cut the blue air
        into papel picado,
a banner of hummingbirds
        on a tissue paper sky.

At summer's end,
        green gems
with mango throats
        rested on elm twigs
between battles
        for the sugar feeder.
Their hearts raced
        like pencil points
tapping out
        furious poems.

On my altar
        lie strewn the last
of your letters.
        Some trill in the shells
of their envelopes,
        others pour a gleam
of verse,
        fiery marigold petals
that mark paths
        for the dead.

Outside, a sudden wind
        scatters the memory
of summer birds.
        Your words seek
a similar departure—
        but the leaf of my heart,
yet glowing,
        does not let go.

Epiphany

Galls adorn the live oaks
that all summer
devoted their own sugar
to grow homes for wasps.

In my lap,
a box of ornaments
bought the year I was pregnant
with my daughter.

Within each gall,
a daughter folds herself
from larva to wasp.
Eggs grow in her belly
made fertile by
insect annunciation.

Wood angel with refined hands,
songbird of painted clay,
bright French horn
and animals of Africa.

In January,
a tiny goddess
emerges from the gall
and basks in the thin blue milk
of the sun's rays.

Each bauble is a memory
in the evergreen of my heart.
I feel again
how my daughter
leans into the light.

Ceremony for the Cynipid Wasp

Gather wasp galls beneath an oak,
rub the raku baubles in your palm.

Peer inside the cynipid wasp's
exit hole, a perfect "o." Marvel at

the labor of her jaws. If no spider
has claimed the gall as home,

crush the hard beads, soak the shards,
distill the tannins into ink.

Wild bees sipped nectar that seeped
to the gall's mottled skin

while inside, a pale larva folded herself
into a hunchbacked wasp.

These live in the ink when you dip
your brush and trace a circle

to praise cynipid's exit,
her entrance into light.

Flight Surgeon

Startled, owl snaps from a perch
in the woolen dark. My feet lift
in surprise, ankles sprout wings.

An arc of silence passes overhead,
a cloud of white feathers so close,
the ends of my hair untether.

Was her conversion like this—the surgeon
who tossed her diploma in a basket
and went to work in the hospital laundry?

When first I heard, I protested
the dulling of her scalpel, the talons
of her learning. Was it madness?

Inspired medicine? Sheets tenderly
folded gave wings to every bed. Pillows
became the downy breasts of swans.

Cranes at Aransas Pass: Quilt Square for 350.org

The needle's slim body
skims currents of cloth,

a folded Japanese handkerchief
in which blue crabs scurry.

A remnant of red silk
warms the backs

of three whooping cranes—
sunrise in Aransas Refuge.

The voice of needle through silk
is the sound of marsh grass
ruffled by sea breeze,

through cotton, the sound
of feathers dipped in black night
folded over snow-white backs.

This is the sound of rest
after long migration,

the murmur of shallow tides
against slender ankles,

the ease attained
after fierce and improbable effort.

This is the last wild flock
of whooping cranes

whose fidelity of flight
binds salt marsh and boreal forest.

Here, held in my hands
against a rising sea.

Early Morning Runs that Became Rescues

1

A young opossum hit by car, four dead babies strewn about her like spokes of a wheel. I lifted the four survivors, bewildered and squirming. Folded my shirt into a pouch and tucked them in.

2

A nighthawk with broken wing crouched in speckled grasses. As I lifted her, dark eyes swallowed me, tiny beak opened to a wide bell.

3

Heart froze, then sped—buck hanging from a spear-tipped fence. Pierced groin, haunches wedged, thread of breath fading. I roused neighbors. We heaved him up and over. He bounded, leapt. He lived.

4

A hiss like castanets stopped me, the false rattle of a bull snake tangled in garden webbing. Praise the keeled scales that excited my hands. I cut him free.

One Hundred Thousand, 2003

The president said,
"I am a patient man,"
when asked how many years
of occupation
could be expected in Iraq.

The world held the bricks
of King Nebuchadnezzar patient.
For 2,600 years they lined Babylon
but now lie scattered and broken.

The defense secretary explained,
It is not our policy
to report civilian deaths.

The count was left to mothers
who bathed the bodies,
intimate one last time
with elbow, small of back, silenced lips.
Keening the names of sons and daughters,
Girls who answered to names that meant
Garden, Deer, and Star
Jenan   Maha   Najma
Boys called Beauty, Quiet, Wise
Jamal   Aram   Hakim

Sesame Seeds Pray

May you burn us to make soot for ink,
a calligraphy of caves filled with treasure.

Make of us a unit to measure the square
root of two, the diagonal of a holy brick.

Tap our pods: we are locks clicking open
        iftah ya simsim
        open sesame

Open us.

Press us for oil, ferment us into wine.
Sprinkle your breads, season your soups.

Take comfort in our earth-colored coats.
buff. tan. gold. brown. red. gray. black.
We are little thrones of health.

We are seeds of reconciliation. We are
your oldest. Mix us with honey and cumin.

Empathy for the Diamond Ant

Incised glass
jeweler's cut on crystal
this tidy geometry of ant
the hue of sherry
that floats to the top
of the glass when I fill it
with water.

She is hunched over
as if holding an
invisible globe,
curled in a death
not recent.

Surprised, my eyes
trace her anatomy,
this intrusion that
starts as a pin prick
then expands
to the swipe of a diamond
across the red fiber
of my heart.

Phantom

The double trunks
of an oak shared a long kiss,
a Rodin embrace in bark.
Lightning struck and one trunk
smoldered to a black shell.
Sap blistered to crust
the color of turmeric,
bright yellow root,
spice to staunch bleeding.

A soldier lost both legs, was placed
on a pile of corpses like a cord of wood,
when he heard a woman's voice plead
Not yet.

His hand reached for the ribbon
of that voice, and he lived.
The voice without a body traveled to him
from the seam between life and death,
woody-scented, pungent.

Ingredients

Last night you called.
I remembered the hours
you and I stole in a zendo's loft
the summer we were students
of the monk who planted plums.
Two strands of incense smoke
braided in and out of each other,
shy in the candle's musk.
The following morning,
in the mild way of buddhas,
we chose friendship instead.

You tell me about your hospice work,
the elderly couple you visit
in the hospital. The husband,
ninety-four years old,
visits his wife every day,
clutching a thermos of fresh soup
he has made for her.
Broths of potato, carrot, and turnip.

I tell you about my father who is
caring for my mother at home.
He invents new dishes
to coax her to eat. Cornish hens,
chopped tomato and raisins.
Dates tucked in the coleslaw.

That summer, years ago,
you and I shared kitchen duty.
The monks were forbidden
onions and garlic.
Your mantra was, "All dishes benefit
from a squeeze of lemon."
Your hands, browned by the sun,
held lemon halves over
every pot, a bit of zest.

Arrival

My mother's mouth
grew round as a coin,
the pallid mouth of a carp
drinking silver water.
Her final breath was a silent catch,
an intake of air only.
The pebble that pulsed at her throat
dropped into a still pond,
and I wondered on what shore
she would release
that last taste of air.

On the tenth day,
I pressed my grief against an oak.
A butterfly appeared,
perched on the dark knuckled bark.
The little wood god,
did I hear his flute of reeds?
When the butterfly,
a common nymph,
opened her skirts,
marbled fawns and ambers,
gold sequins in a cinnamon hem—
it was an out breath,
an arrival.

Sandhill Cranes at Salado Creek

Along the creek's curl
light rain falls.

Snails drag
the wet gravity
of shells.

Birds preen mud
into feathers to blend
with brown grasses.

A millipede of heartbeats,
we run a shared cord
of breath.

Then! ears shake
with tumbled ecstasy,
 O bugle and accordion!

Wave and wave
and wave
of shimmering V-lines,

strings of prayer flags,
parents singing children
across the sky.

San Anto Persimmons
    for Emilita

Mother and daughter, because you walk
beneath the summer sun in a state
of adoration, your steps slow and light,

come eat the black plums of my body; rest
your cheeks against my smooth skin
peeled to shades of dove and primrose.

Press your ears to the polish of my trunk,
and listen to the ebony wood of my heart
where mandolins are sleeping.

Watch my palette of fruit as it ripens,
astringent green to sweet jammy black,
the way the deepening years pledge you

to the earth and bind you to each other.

During the City Nature Challenge

One hundred forty-five species in four days.
I have learned Venus' Looking Glass, curled dock,
yellow stonecrop, heartleaf nettle.
On the last day I watch two
iridescent green bottleflies
feast on the flesh of a dead bird.
And high overhead, a kettle of hawks
ride thermals in an open sky.

Once fifteen pounds, now nine,
my cat's body announces every bone,
jutting ribs, his spine a ladder.
Still, he purrs and cuddles, bosses the dog,
not yet ready to leave his indoor meadow.
At night, he sleeps in the curl of my body.

The seed baskets of Mexican prickly poppies
are star-shaped and thorny, brimming
with seeds. A huge nectar fly,
obsidian black, rests on a glass shard
in the street— a Mexican cactus fly.
Mockingbirds sing arias on telephone poles.

It is cancer, and the vet prescribes
chemo compounded in Arizona,
delivered on a block of ice.
Warned to wear disposable gloves,
my hands turn alien
each time I coax the syringe
into his mouth, a barrier of
plastic between us.

Stalks of blue lettuce soar to eight feet;
Texas sedge makes a tufted carpet
around the birdbath where grackles splash.
Wild garlic dances beside coastal germander,
and an orb weaver rests on a salvia leaf.

As a young cat, he spent hours tracking
and pouncing at luminous geckos
that hunted moths on the other side
of a glass window.
We joked it was a cat's video game.

My yard proves rich in vines:
pearl milkweed, creeping cucumber,
a tangle of Virgin's Bower. Snailseed
and sorrel vine. Curtain of Mustang Grape.
White-winged doves feast on the
flat black seeds of dayflower.

The house is the only landscape he knows,
a maze of closets, cupboards and
cardboard boxes, the mossy hang
of blankets over beds. He likes to rest
his head against the laptop.

I participate in the City Nature Challenge,
four days of snapping photos for iNaturalist
in my backyard,
the few lots not yet built on,
along green belts and drainage ditches,
at the edges of road.

Thirteen years ago, I spotted a kitten
while driving home from
Master Naturalist training.
He was barreling down a busy road,
a darling, green-eyed tabby,
thin and scuffed and sniffling.
His paws did not touch real dirt again.
He was an indoor cat because cats kill.
Birds. Billions every year.

*One hundred forty-five species in four days.
I have learned Venus' Looking Glass, curled dock,
yellow stonecrop, heartleaf nettle.
On the last day I watch two
iridescent green bottleflies
feast on the flesh of a dead bird.
And high overhead, a kettle of hawks
ride thermals in an open sky.*

Summer Tomatoes

Sunlight flows
through tree shadow
to touch the garden.
Pulled by the gravity
of ripening tomatoes,
light alters into life,
an altar.

Inhale air's magic,
quaff water at the root,
dangle stars
of yellow blossom.

Each flower
is a fearless diver,
a needle that pulls
a green knot
into place,
sloughs the wilted robe
to give way
to fruit's crescendo.

Curled in the arm
of summer light,
feel the plumb bob
of your own heart
drop you into place
so you, too, may
surge to fullness.

Mole Negro de Oaxaca
    (after Portrait with Monkeys, Frida Kahlo 1943)

Before you sat here, long before you were
held in the soft black arms of monkeys,
their spidery fingers a blessing over your heart,

songbirds plucked chile pequins, those red
little grandmothers of all chiles. They carried
them in their gullets and dropped the seeds

over Azteca lands. Each tint of soil coaxed seed
in new directions: pasilla or chipotle,
guajillo and ancho, your favorite-chilhuacles.

I can see it in your eyes, your proud back,
you have roasted and soaked the chiles,
measured pumpkin seed, anise, and raisin.

You have broken bitter chocolate into pieces
to mix with your own tears.
You have counted cinnamon sticks and cloves

and tossed the colors of your laughter
into the cast iron pot. The aroma of
mole negro de Oaxaca enters the garden.

Soon, you will rise and announce the day's
fiestas. From the earth of your heart,
we will be fed.

Spira Mirabilis

A white snail, globular drop,
crawls up the smooth trunk
of a persimmon tree.
She tucks her gel body,
mucosal, wet,
into her spiral chamber
and closes a lid
against summer heat.

An equation maps her shell:
logarithmic spiral, polar curve,
the curl of ice on Mars
or spin of water
to halt a forest fire.

Our eyes, too,
tucked in their orbital cribs
trace the galaxy's ribs of fire.
Cells in our own corneas
slide the wondrous spiral.

Small pearl, snail at rest,
hidden cells of vision,
guide us now through drought
and flame and flood.
Turn our course,
return the cooling hand
of love.

Black Rose

In Arizona, only the dead protect Patagonia-eyed silk moths
where a handful still live on a half-acre cemetery
not yet claimed by grazing cattle or climate chaos.
Species after species vanish.

We carry outrage and grief to the plaza to protest the caging
of children torn from mothers' arms,
fleeing bullets, hunger, drought.
Trapped like moths in a cemetery. Forced
to sleep on concrete floors. No windows to the sky.
Childhood vanishes.

A cocoon is not a cage but a cradle.

This morning, four rattles the color of bone dangle
by single loops of silk on twigs of Texas sage.
I am held spellbound by the cocoon of a calleta silk moth.

The ghosts of my hands slip into her sleeping vessel where
she is curled and pulsing. A trellis of insect bone holds
the black rose she is becoming.
I know I rest in the temple of an elder
who knows how to spin a new body, how to make of a mind a flower.
Molecules paint a stripe of moonlight across her developing wings,
circle her velvet body with a wine-red collar.

A cocoon is not a cage but a cradle.

I tuck my human frailty inside of her, knowing we have come
from a common ancestor who gave us symmetry of wing and limb,
a desire to freely move, an urge to continue life.

Some night she will awaken. The spread of her black wings
will be soft as petals, her nuptial flight will shift the season
and shake the stars. Come, she will say, *it is not too late.*
Break open the cages. Make of our World a Cradle.

Mobi Warren is a poet, translator, and retired math educator from San Antonio, Texas. She studied Ancient Greek at the University of Texas at Austin and holds a Master of Arts degree in Multidisciplinary Sciences from the University of the Incarnate Word. In 1977, she sailed the South China Sea with a project to rescue Vietnamese refugees, the "boat people," and she is the translator, from the Vietnamese, of several books by Zen Master Thich Nhat Hanh, including *The Miracle of Mindfulness*.

Warren has worked as a professional storyteller and puppeteer in an art museum and has taught mathematics to all grades from kindergarten to high school seniors. She is the author of a science fiction/time travel novel for young people, *The Bee Maker*, that concerns endangered honeybees and was a 2019 finalist for both the Jean Flynn Award for Best Middle Grade Book and the Gertrude Warner Award for Middle Grade Fiction. Warren is a Texas Master Naturalist, native plants enthusiast, and lover of insects who volunteers as a citizen scientist helping to gather data on Monarch butterflies and other pollinators.

Warren leads poetry hikes in natural areas in the San Antonio region and offers workshops through the literary arts organization Gemini Ink, including a class *The Poet as Citizen Scientist*. She is the co-founder of *Stone in the Stream/Roca en el Rio*, a regional collective of Texas writers and visual artists committed to environmental protection and climate justice through contemplative, artistic, and activist response.

More about her work and puppets can be found at https://mobiwarren.com.

www.ingramcontent.com/pod-product-compliance
Lightning Source LLC
LaVergne TN
LVHW040117080426
835507LV00041B/1452